ALABAMA CRIMSON TIDE

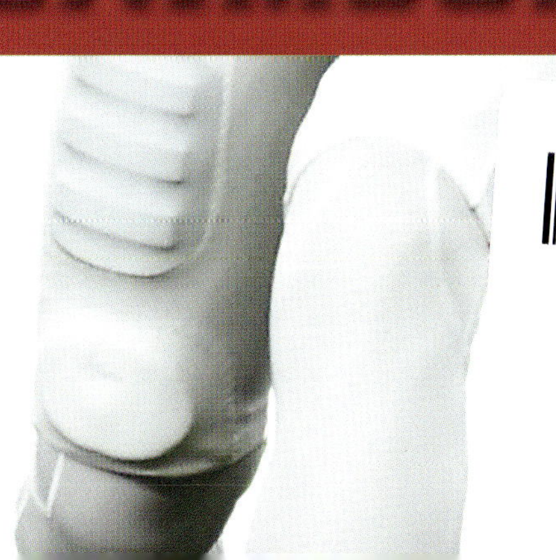

CHARLIE BEATTIE

WWW.APEXEDITIONS.COM

Apex is distributed by North Star Editions:
sales@northstareditions.com | 888-417-0195

Produced for Apex by Red Line Editorial.

Photographs ©: Jose/MarinMedia.org/Cal Sport Media/ZUMA Press Wire/AP Images, cover, 1; Robert Sutton/The Tuscaloosa News/AP Images, 4–5; Butch Dill/AP Images, 6–7, 58–59; Shutterstock Images, 8–9, 37, 50–51, 52–53, 54–55; Bettmann/Getty Images, 10–11, 19, 24–25, 26–27; AP Images, 12–13, 16–17, 22–23; Horace Cort/AP Images, 14–15; Sporting News/Getty Images, 20–21; Rick Bowmer/AP Images, 28–29; Chris Graythen/Getty Images Sport/Getty Images, 30–31; Mike Ehrmann/Getty Images Sport/Getty Images, 32–33; Peter McMahon/Miami Dolphins/AP Images, 34–35, 57; Tom Hauck/Getty Images Sport/Getty Images, 38–39; Kevin C. Cox/Getty Images Sport/Getty Images, 40–41, 42–43, 47; Wesley Hitt/Getty Images Sport/Getty Images, 44–45; Sean Gardner/Getty Images Sport/Getty Images, 48–49

Library of Congress Control Number: 2025930331

ISBN
979-8-89250-710-3 (hardcover)
979-8-89250-762-2 (paperback)
979-8-89250-745-5 (ebook pdf)
979-8-89250-728-8 (hosted ebook)

Printed in the United States of America
Mankato, MN
082025

NOTE TO PARENTS AND EDUCATORS

Apex books are designed to build literacy skills in striving readers. Exciting, high-interest content attracts and holds readers' attention. The text is carefully leveled to allow students to achieve success quickly.

TABLE OF CONTENTS

CHAPTER 1

ROLL TIDE!

It's two hours before game time at the University of Alabama. Fans line up along the Walk of Champions. This pathway leads to Bryant–Denny Stadium. Soon, Alabama's coaches and players arrive.

Alabama players arrive at the stadium two to three hours before each game.

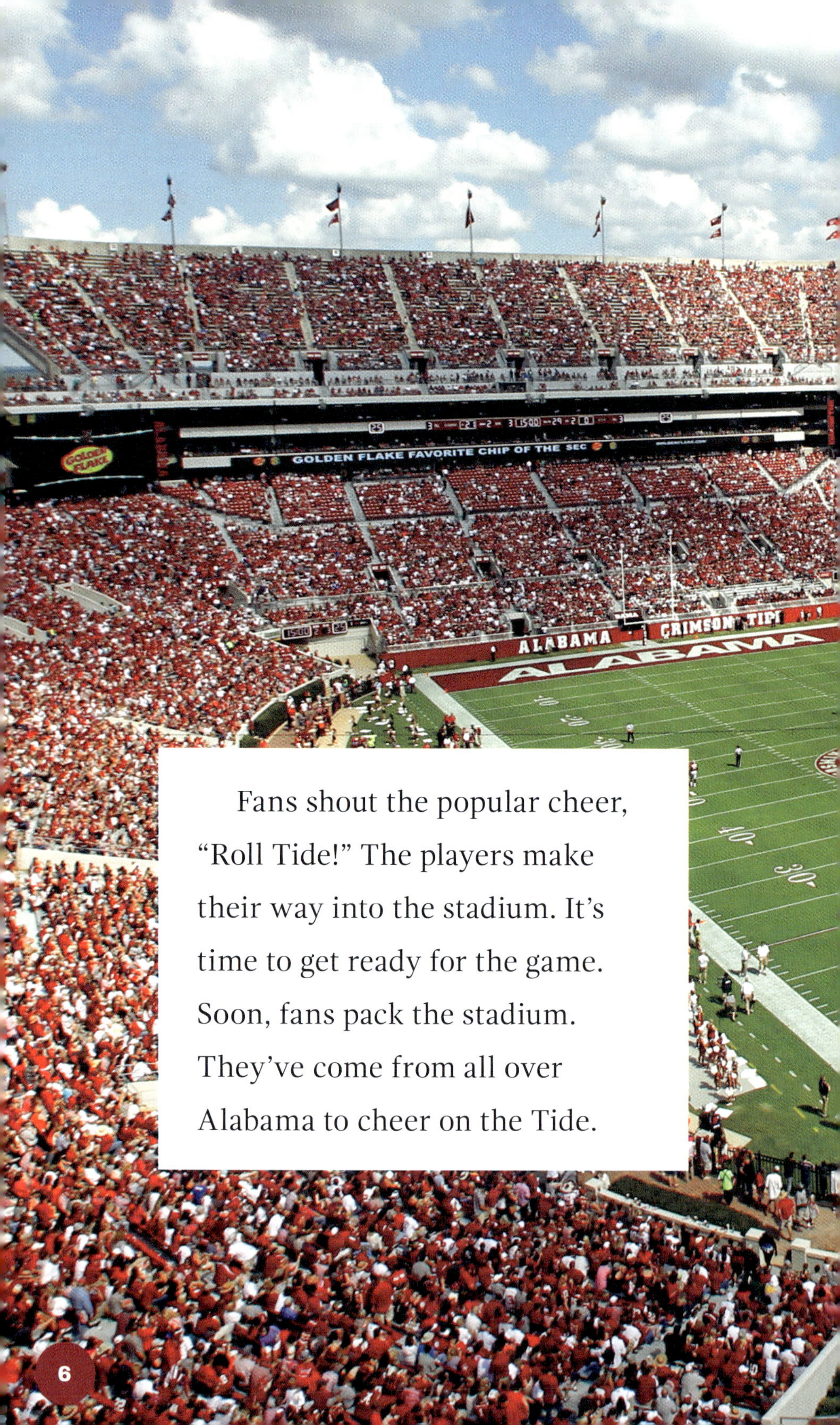

Fans shout the popular cheer, "Roll Tide!" The players make their way into the stadium. It's time to get ready for the game. Soon, fans pack the stadium. They've come from all over Alabama to cheer on the Tide.

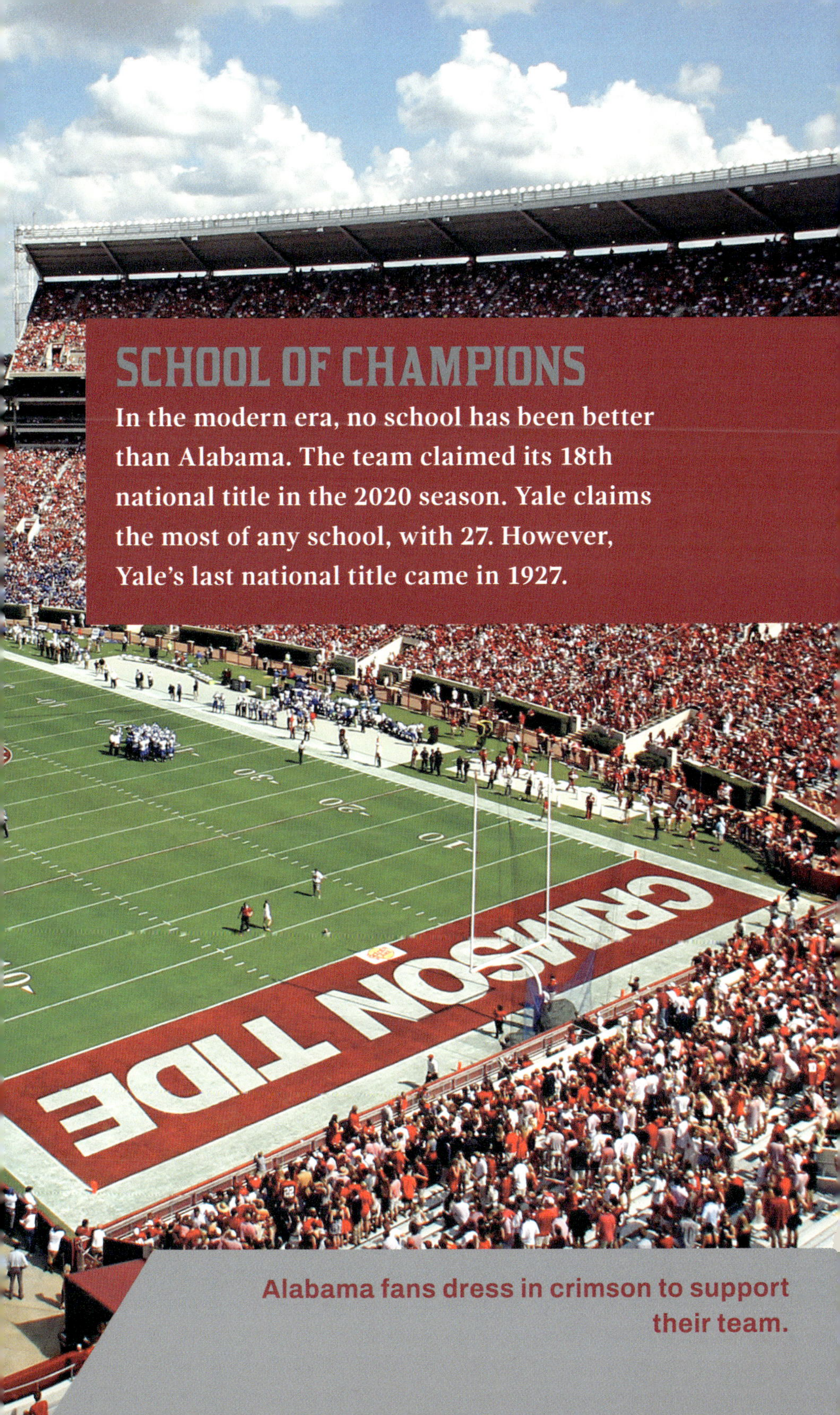

SCHOOL OF CHAMPIONS

In the modern era, no school has been better than Alabama. The team claimed its 18th national title in the 2020 season. Yale claims the most of any school, with 27. However, Yale's last national title came in 1927.

Alabama fans dress in crimson to support their team.

CHAPTER 2

EARLY HISTORY

Alabama's football team formed in 1892. Back then, fans called the team the Thin Red Line. But in 1907, Alabama played Auburn on a muddy field. The red mud stained Alabama's white uniforms. A reporter called the team the Crimson Tide. The name stuck.

By 2024, more than 40,000 students attended the University of Alabama.

Wallace Wade coached Alabama until 1930.

Wallace Wade became the team's head coach in 1923. He turned Alabama into a power. The Tide played in the Rose Bowl three times. They won it in the 1925 and 1930 seasons.

GAINING RESPECT

In the 1920s, many football fans didn't think Southern teams were very good. But in the 1925 season, Alabama beat an excellent Washington team in the Rose Bowl. The 20–19 win made fans take notice. Soon, Alabama and other Southern schools gained respect.

When Wade left, Frank Thomas became the new head coach. In 1934, Thomas led Alabama to an undefeated season. The Tide beat Stanford in the Rose Bowl. Alabama claimed a national title that season.

RUN FOR THE ROSES

The Tide played in the Rose Bowl six times between 1926 and 1946. They went 4–1–1. They didn't play in the famous game again until 2024. That year, Alabama lost to Michigan in the playoff.

Alabama scores a touchdown against Stanford in the Rose Bowl.

Alabama struggled in the 1950s. Former player Paul "Bear" Bryant took over as head coach. He quickly turned Alabama around. Bryant's teams claimed three national titles in the 1960s.

In the 1961 season, Alabama (dark jerseys) beat Arkansas 10–3 in the Sugar Bowl.

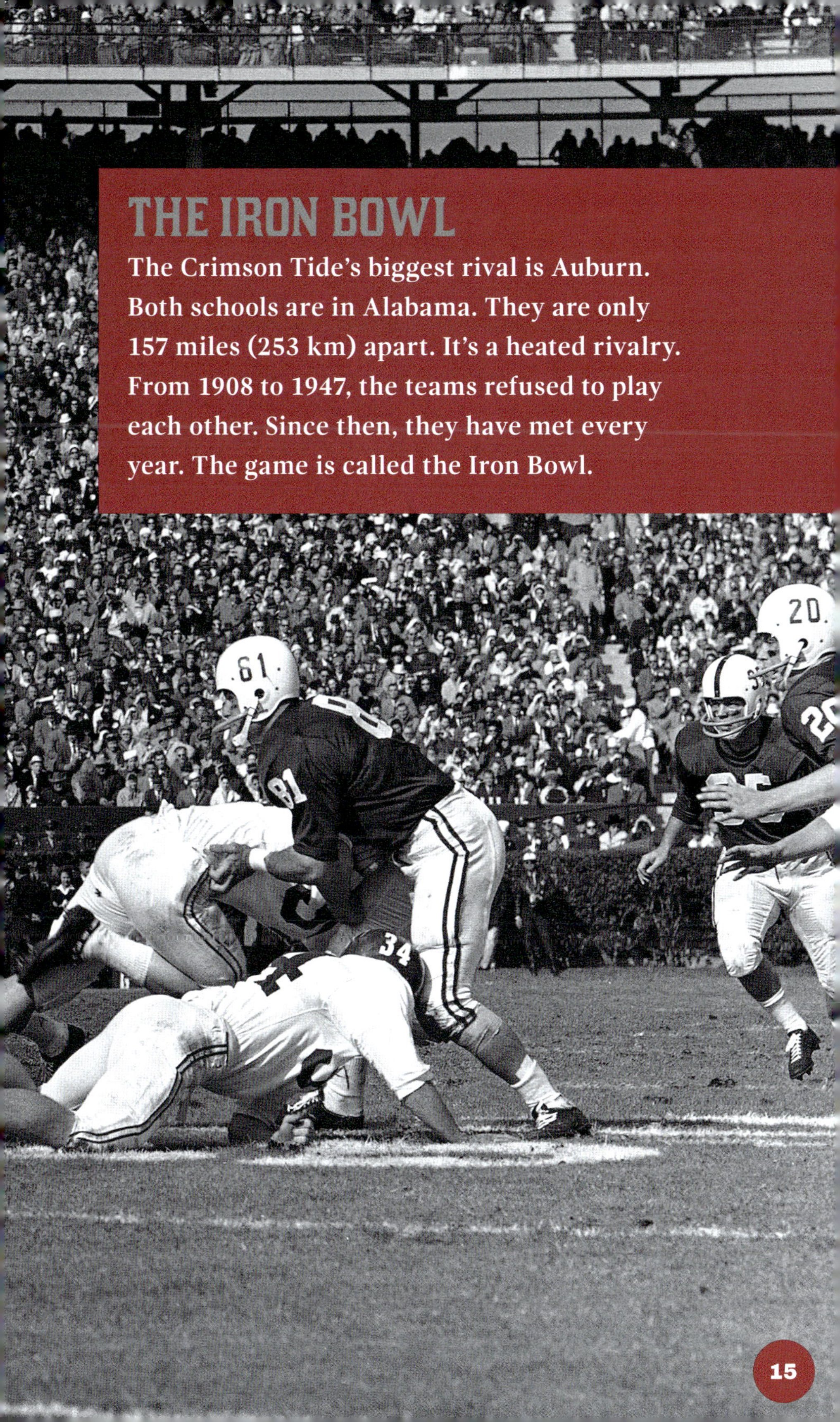

THE IRON BOWL

The Crimson Tide's biggest rival is Auburn. Both schools are in Alabama. They are only 157 miles (253 km) apart. It's a heated rivalry. From 1908 to 1947, the teams refused to play each other. Since then, they have met every year. The game is called the Iron Bowl.

Alabama's defense lifted the Tide to a Sugar Bowl victory in the 1978 season.

Bryant won three more national titles in the 1970s. He loved coaching Alabama. He often said he couldn't live without it. Bryant retired after the 1982 season. Four weeks later, he died at the age of 69.

GOAL LINE STAND

In the 1978 season, Alabama played Penn State in the Sugar Bowl. The Tide needed to win to become national champs. In the fourth quarter, Alabama's defense stopped Penn State at the goal line. The stand secured a 14–7 win.

COACH SPOTLIGHT

BEAR BRYANT

Paul "Bear" Bryant played for Alabama from 1931 to 1934. Before the 1958 season, the school hired him as head coach. Bryant ran hard practices. Many players quit the team. But the ones who stuck around became tough.

Bryant led the Tide to 24 bowl games. Alabama also won six national titles under Bryant.

BEAR BRYANT WENT 232–46–9 IN HIS 25 YEARS WITH ALABAMA.

Bryant was known for his signature look. He wore a houndstooth hat on the sideline. Today, many fans wear these hats to games. They honor the legendary coach.

CHAPTER 3

LEGENDS

Johnny Mack Brown was blazing fast. The running back led the way in the 1925 season. In the Rose Bowl, he raced past the Washington defense for two touchdowns. The scores helped Alabama win its first national title.

Johnny Mack Brown led Alabama to a perfect record in the 1925 season.

Dixie Howell didn't just run and throw. He was also a great punter.

Dixie Howell and Don Hutson starred for the Crimson Tide in 1934. Howell played halfback. He threw most of Alabama's passes. Hutson was one of the best receivers of his time. The Howell-to-Hutson connection led Alabama to an undefeated record.

THE FIRST HERO

Auxford Burks became known as Alabama's "First Great Halfback Hero." He starred for the Tide from 1902 to 1906. When Burks graduated, one fan wrote a poem called "Farewell to Burks."

Bear Bryant said Joe Namath was the best athlete he'd ever coached. Namath played for Alabama from 1962 to 1964. In that time, his accurate passing led the team to a 29–4 record. The Tide won the national title in Namath's final season.

Joe Namath (12) threw for 756 yards in 1964.

BREAKING BARRIERS

For many years, Alabama didn't allow Black players. That finally changed in 1971. Defensive end John Mitchell became an All-American in 1972. He also served as a team captain.

After graduating in 1972, John Hannah became the fourth overall pick in the NFL Draft.

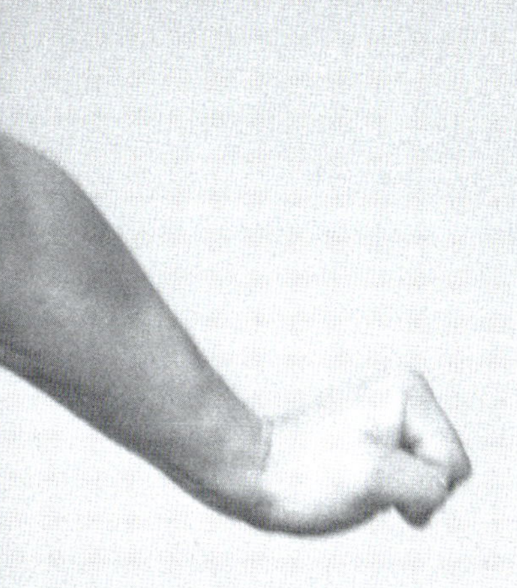

Bryant loved to run the ball. To do that, he needed good linemen. In the 1970s, John Hannah and Dwight Stephenson were two of the best. The powerful Hannah also won a wrestling championship at Alabama. He was a track and field star, too.

TOP LINEBACKERS

Alabama has had many great linebackers. In the 1970s, Woodrow Lowe earned All-America honors three times. Cornelius Bennett matched that feat in the 1980s. Derrick Thomas loved to punish opposing quarterbacks. Between 1985 and 1988, Thomas racked up 52 sacks. No one in school history has more.

CHAPTER 4

RECENT HISTORY

By 1992, Alabama hadn't won a national title since Bear Bryant left. That year, the Crimson Tide broke the streak. Alabama finished 12–0 under coach Gene Stallings. The Tide thumped Miami 34–13 in the Sugar Bowl. They were voted the top team in the nation.

Alabama safety George Teague returns an interception for a touchdown in the Sugar Bowl.

Nick Saban became Alabama's coach in 2007. Two years later, the team finished 14–0. That included a thrilling win over rival Auburn. Then Alabama played Texas in the national title game. The Tide rolled to a 37–21 win.

Saban's teams continued to dominate. In 2011, Alabama beat rival LSU 21–0 in the national title game. The Tide won again the next season. This time, they crushed Notre Dame 42–14.

In 2009, Mark Ingram ran for 1,658 yards and 17 touchdowns.

Quarterback Tua Tagovailoa (13) threw three touchdown passes in the national title game of the 2017 season.

The Crimson Tide reached the national title game once again in the 2015 season. Alabama faced Clemson. The game went back and forth. But the Tide won 45–40. That started an amazing run. Alabama reached six title games in seven years.

OVERTIME DRAMA

In the 2017 season, Alabama faced Georgia in the title game. The Tide trailed 20–7 in the third quarter. But Alabama rallied to force overtime. Quarterback Tua Tagovailoa hit receiver DeVonta Smith on a 41-yard touchdown pass. Alabama won a 26–23 thriller.

Alabama won the title again in 2020. This time, the Tide smashed Ohio State 52–20. The win finished off a perfect 13–0 season. Saban left after the 2023 season. New coach Kalen DeBoer took over. He had big shoes to fill.

RIVALRY DAYS

Some of Alabama's biggest rivalry games are played on the same weekend every year. The Tide play Tennessee on the third Saturday in October. They play LSU on the first Saturday in November. And they play Auburn the Saturday after Thanksgiving.

DeVonta Smith scored three touchdowns in the title game of the 2020 season.

COACH SPOTLIGHT

NICK SABAN

Crimson Tide fans once rooted against Nick Saban. From 2000 to 2004, he coached LSU. However, Alabama hired him in 2007. And he quickly became a success.

Saban turned Alabama into the best team in college football. He led the Tide to six national titles. That was equal to the great Bear Bryant.

Saban won 88 percent of his games with the Tide. The school decided to honor him. The field at Bryant–Denny Stadium became known as Nick Saban Field.

NICK SABAN WON 206 GAMES DURING HIS TIME AT ALABAMA.

CHAPTER 5

MODERN STARS

Chris Samuels was a dominant blocker. The powerful tackle played for Alabama from 1996 to 1999. In 42 games, he never allowed a sack. Samuels also opened holes for running back Shaun Alexander. In 1999, Alexander earned SEC Player of the Year honors. He led the nation with 23 touchdowns that year.

In 1999, Shaun Alexander led the SEC with 1,383 rushing yards.

In 2014, Amari Cooper led the nation with 124 catches.

Alabama has had many great running backs. In 2009, Mark Ingram became the first Alabama player to win the Heisman Trophy. That award goes to the best player in college football.

Alabama has also produced great receivers. Amari Cooper recorded 1,727 receiving yards in 2014. That set a school record. DeVonta Smith broke that mark in 2020. Smith won the Heisman that season.

TALENTED CLASS

Many great pro players come from Alabama. In 2021, six members of the Crimson Tide were drafted in the first round. That tied a record for the most first-round picks from one school.

In 2021, Bryce Young set an Alabama record with 47 touchdown passes in a season.

Nick Saban's teams had great quarterbacks, too. Jalen Hurts could win games with his arm or his legs. Tua Tagovailoa threw accurate passes. And in 2021, Bryce Young became the first Alabama quarterback to win the Heisman.

RECORD SMASHER

A. J. McCarron was Alabama's starting quarterback in the early 2010s. In his four years with the team, he threw for 9,019 yards. That made him the school's all-time leader. McCarron won 36 games during his career. He lost only four.

Defensive tackle Terrence Cody was huge. Some fans called him "Mount Cody." He was known for blocking kicks. Jonathan Allen was another dominant defensive tackle. He recorded more than 150 tackles. Will Anderson Jr. knew how to take down quarterbacks. In 2021, he led the nation with 17.5 sacks.

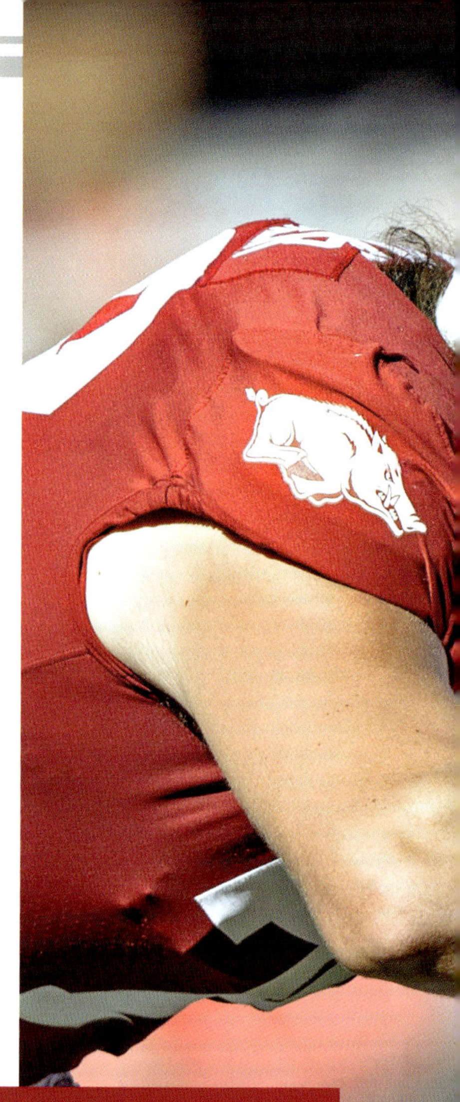

MINKAH'S PICKS

Defensive back Minkah Fitzpatrick intercepted two passes in 2015. Both picks were in the same game. And he ran both back for touchdowns. Fitzpatrick ran back another pick for a score in 2016. This one was 100 yards. It was the longest interception return in Alabama history.

Will Anderson Jr. was named the nation's best defensive player in 2022.

PLAYER SPOTLIGHT

DERRICK HENRY

Taking down Derrick Henry wasn't easy. The running back was huge. He pounded defenders. Then he kept going for big gains.

In 2015, Henry became the Tide's starting back. He topped 200 yards four times. Henry was at his best in the biggest games. He exploded for 271 yards against Auburn. He also shined in the national title game. He had 158 yards and three touchdowns. Henry won the Heisman Trophy that season.

IN 2015, DERRICK HENRY LED THE NATION WITH 2,219 RUSHING YARDS AND 28 TOUCHDOWNS.

BAMA

CHAPTER 6

TEAM TRIVIA

In 2022, Alabama won the Sugar Bowl 45–20 over Kansas State. It was the Crimson Tide's 46th bowl win. No team has won more. Alabama's total includes three wins in the national title game between 2009 and 2012. It also includes three playoff wins between 2016 and 2020.

Kobe Prentice scores a touchdown during a 45–20 win over Kansas State in the 2022 Sugar Bowl.

Alabama's simple, classic look is famous throughout college football.

Some college teams update their uniforms often. But Alabama's uniforms have not changed since 1985. The team's crimson helmets are unique. Each helmet features the player's number. The school began the tradition in 1957.

PACKING 'EM IN

Bryant–Denny Stadium holds 100,077 fans. The city of Tuscaloosa has just under 112,000 people. When it's full, Bryant–Denny would be the fifth-largest city in the state of Alabama.

Big Al often waves an Alabama flag to pump up the crowd before games.

In 1930, a reporter wrote about Alabama's big players. He compared them to a herd of elephants. Soon, the school started using an elephant as its mascot. Since 1980, a student has worn a costume. He's known as Big Al.

FAMOUS CHANT

The yellowhammer is the state bird of Alabama. Tide fans work the bird's name into a chant. It's known as the "Rammer Jammer" cheer. The chant includes the line "Rammer Jammer, Yellowhammer!"

The Million Dollar Band plays at every Alabama home game.

After a loss in 1922, a reporter asked an Alabama coach why the team had struggled. The coach said the school had a million-dollar band. That meant there was no money left to support a good team. The band started using that name.

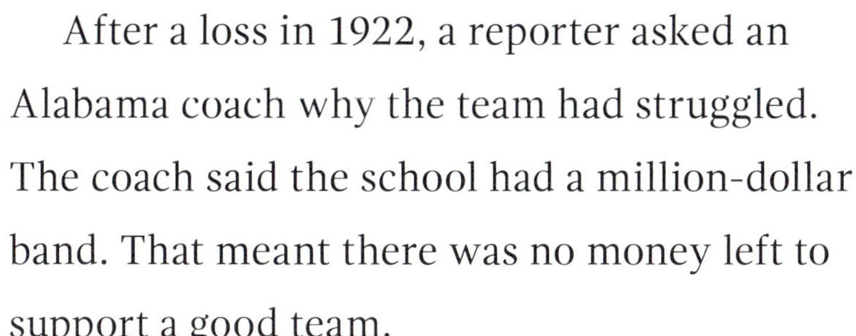

SWEET HOME ALABAMA

Alabama rarely lost at home under Bear Bryant. Between 1963 and 1982, the Tide won 57 straight home games. Bryant finished with a 72–2 record in Tuscaloosa.

TEAM RECORDS

All-Time Passing Yards: **9,019**

A. J. McCarron (2010–13)

All-Time Rushing Yards: **3,843**

Najee Harris (2017–20)

All-Time Receiving Yards: **3,965**

DeVonta Smith (2017–20)

All-Time Touchdowns: **57**

Najee Harris (2017–20)

All-Time Scoring: **547**

Will Reichard (2019–23)

All-Time Interceptions: **19**

Antonio Langham (1990–93)

All-Time Tackles: **327**

Wayne Davis (1983–86)

All-Time Coaching Wins: **232**

Bear Bryant (1958–82)

Heisman Trophy Winners: **4**

Mark Ingram (2009), Derrick Henry (2015), DeVonta Smith (2020), Bryce Young (2021)

National Championships: **18**

1925, 1926†, 1930†, 1934†, 1941†, 1961†, 1964†, 1965†, 1973†, 1978†, 1979, 1992, 2009, 2011, 2012, 2015, 2017, 2020

† *Season in which more than one school claims the national title.*

All statistics are accurate through 2024.

BAMA
SEC
GRADUATE
2021

TIMELINE

1892
Alabama forms its first football team.

1926
On January 1, the Crimson Tide win their first Rose Bowl by beating Washington 20–19.

1958
Paul "Bear" Bryant begins his first season as Alabama's head coach.

1979
On January 1, Bryant wins his sixth national title after Alabama beats Penn State 14–7 in the Sugar Bowl.

1993
After beating Miami 34–13 in the Sugar Bowl on January 1, Alabama wins its first national title in 14 years.

2007

2009

2013

2018

2024

Alabama hires Nick Saban as head coach.

Mark Ingram becomes the first Alabama player to win the Heisman Trophy.

On January 7, Alabama wins the national title for the third time in four years by beating Notre Dame 42–14.

On January 8, Tua Tagovailoa's 41-yard pass to DeVonta Smith in overtime gives Alabama another national title.

Nick Saban retires as head coach after leading the Crimson Tide to six titles in 17 seasons.

COMPREHENSION QUESTIONS

Write your answers on a separate piece of paper.

1. Write a paragraph that explains the main ideas of Chapter 4.
2. Who do you think was the greatest player in Alabama history? Why?
3. What was Alabama's football team known as before 1907?
   - A. the Crimson Elephants
   - B. the Yellowhammers
   - C. the Thin Red Line
4. Why did Kalen DeBoer have big shoes to fill when he became Alabama's coach?
   - A. Alabama no longer had good players on the team.
   - B. The previous coach won six national titles.
   - C. Many fans stopped going to Alabama's games.

5. What does **graduated** mean in this book?

He starred for the Tide from 1902 to 1906. When Burks ***graduated****, one fan wrote a poem called "Farewell to Burks."*

A. finished school
B. scored a touchdown
C. wrote something down

6. What does **unique** mean in this book?

The team's crimson helmets are ***unique****. Each helmet features the player's number.*

A. different from all others
B. difficult to wear
C. not safe to use

Answer key on page 64.

GLOSSARY

All-America
An honor given to an athlete who is one of the best in the country.

bowl games
Postseason college football games that successful teams are invited to take part in.

captain
The leader of a team.

dominate
To play better than others and win often.

drafted
Chosen by a team when entering a sports league.

mascot
A figure that is the symbol of a sports team.

overtime
An extra period that happens if two teams are tied at the end of the fourth quarter.

retired
Ended one's career.

rival
The opponent that a team has the most intense competition against.

sacks
Plays that happen when a defender tackles the quarterback before he can throw the ball.

tradition
A way of doing something that is passed down over many years.

TO LEARN MORE

BOOKS

Kelley, K. C. *Alabama Crimson Tide.* The Child's World, 2022.

Meier, William. *Alabama Crimson Tide.* Abdo Publishing, 2021.

Streeter, Anthony. *College Football Championship All-Time Greats.* Press Box Books, 2025.

ONLINE RESOURCES

Visit **www.apexeditions.com** to find links and resources related to this title.

ABOUT THE AUTHOR

Charlie Beattie is a writer, editor, and former sportscaster. Originally from Saint Paul, Minnesota, he now lives in Charleston, South Carolina, with his wife and son.

INDEX

ANSWER KEY:

1. Answers will vary; 2. Answers will vary; 3. C; 4. B; 5. A; 6. A